The Urbana Free Library

To renew: call **217-367-4057**
or go to **urbanafreelibrary.org**
and select **My Account**

D1573221

White and Majestic

What Am I?

by Joyce Markovics

Consultant: Eric Darton, Adjunct Faculty
New York University Urban Design and Architecture Studies Program
New York, New York

BEARPORT
PUBLISHING

New York, New York

Credits

Cover, © Vacclav/Shutterstock; 2, © Orhan Cam/Shutterstock; TOC, © Lucky-photographer/iStock; 4–5, © Zoonar GmbH/Alamy; 6–7, © William Perry/Dreamstime; 8–9, © Valerio Rosati/Dreamstime; 10–11, © jiawangkun/Shutterstock; 12–13, © Thomas Woodruff/Dreamstime; 14–15, © Orhan Cam/Shutterstock; 16–17, © dbimages/Alamy; 18–19, © turtix/Shutterstock; 20–21, © turtix/Shutterstock; 22, © S. Borisov/Shutterstock; 23, © Everett Collection/AGE Fotostock; 24, © Joseph Sohm/Shutterstock.

Publisher: Kenn Goin
Senior Editor: Joyce Tavolacci
Creative Director: Spencer Brinker
Design: Debrah Kaiser
Photo Researcher: Thomas Persano

Library of Congress Cataloging-in-Publication Data

Names: Markovics, Joyce L., author.
Title: White and majestic : what am I? / by Joyce Markovics.
Description: New York, New York : Bearport Publishing, 2018. | Series: American place puzzlers series | Includes bibliographical references and index.
Identifiers: LCCN 2017042964 (print) | LCCN 2017046511 (ebook) | ISBN 9781684025435 (ebook) | ISBN 9781684024858 (library)
Subjects: LCSH: White House (Washington, D.C.)—Juvenile literature. | Washington (D.C.)—Buildings, structures, etc.—Juvenile literature. | Presidents—United States—Juvenile literature.
Classification: LCC F204.W5 (ebook) | LCC F204.W5 M275 2018 (print) | DDC 975.3—dc23
LC record available at https://lccn.loc.gov/2017042964

For more information, write to Bearport Publishing Company, Inc., 45 West 21st Street, Suite 3B, New York, New York 10010. Printed in the United States of America.

10 9 8 7 6 5 4 3 2 1

Contents

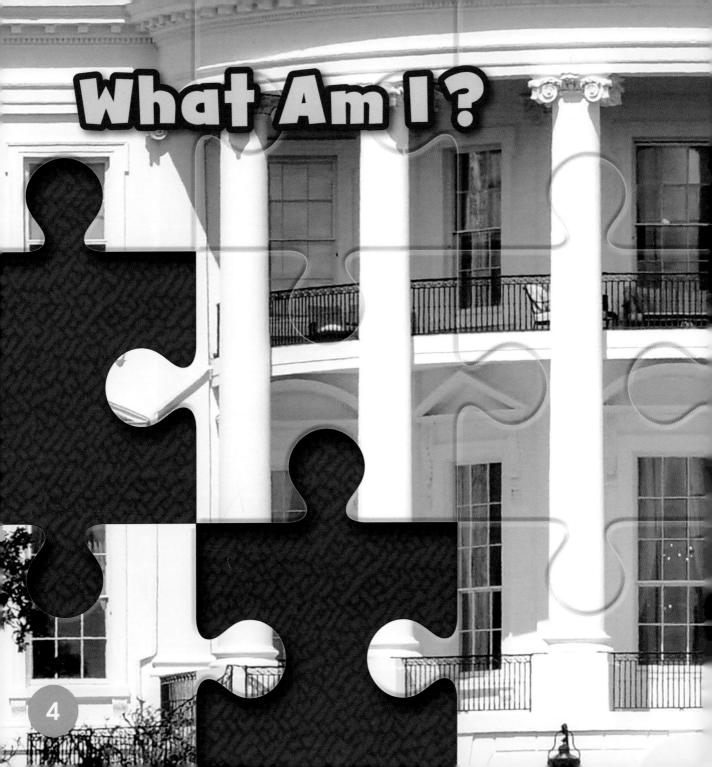

What Am I?

I have tall columns.

A flag flies
from my roof.

6

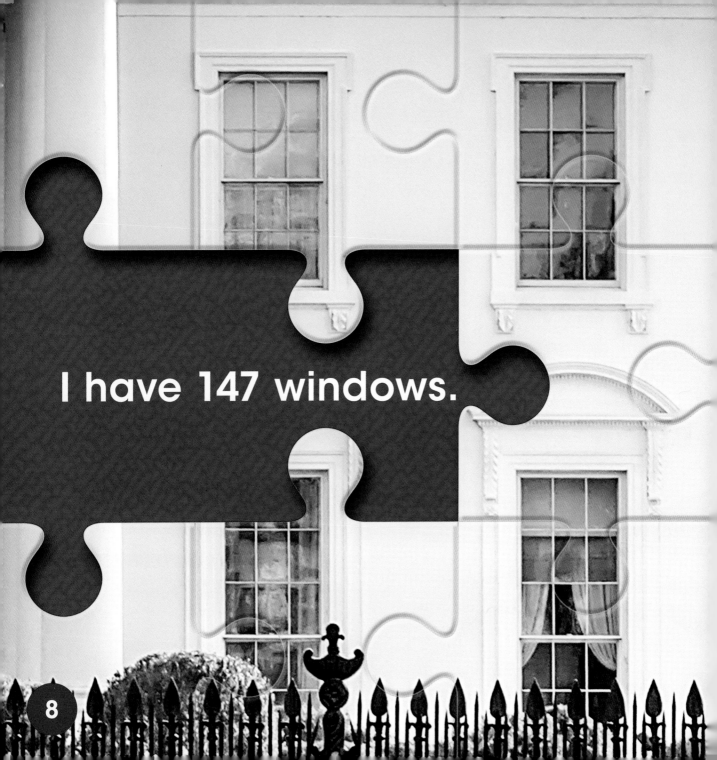

I have 147 windows.

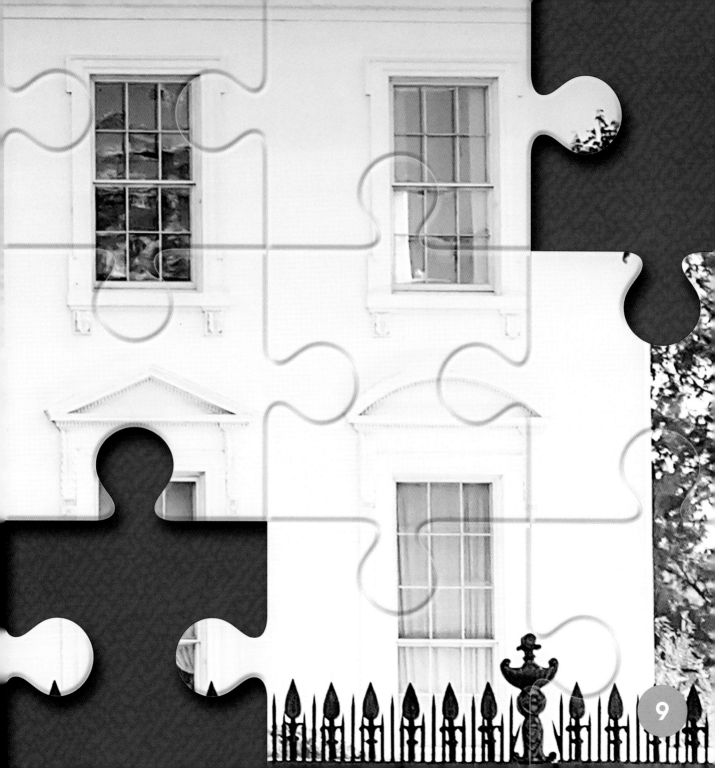

9

A large,
green lawn
surrounds me.

I have an
oval-shaped office.

13

I am painted completely white.

15

The president of the United States calls me home.

What am I?

Let's find out!

19

I am the White House!

Fast Facts

The White House is an important government building and home to the U.S. president. The house was built in 1800.

The White House

Height of Building:	70 feet (21 m)
Length of Building:	168 feet (51 m)
Number of Doors:	412
Number of Rooms:	132
Number of Bathrooms:	35
Cool Fact:	It takes about 570 gallons (2,158 l) of paint to cover the White House.

Where Am I?

The White House is located at 1600 Pennsylvania Avenue in Washington, DC.

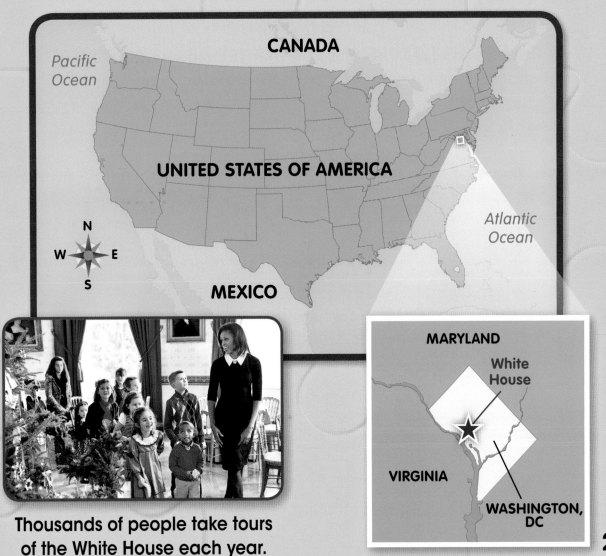

CANADA

Pacific Ocean

UNITED STATES OF AMERICA

Atlantic Ocean

N
W E
S

MEXICO

MARYLAND

White House

VIRGINIA

WASHINGTON, DC

Thousands of people take tours of the White House each year.

Index

Read More

Braithwaite, Jill. *The White House.* Minneapolis, MN: Lerner (2011).

Herrington, Lisa M. *The White House.* New York: Children's Press (2014).

Learn More Online

To learn more about the White House, visit
www.bearportpublishing.com/AmericanPlacePuzzlers

About the Author

Joyce Markovics lives in a very old house along the Hudson River. She's never been to the White House—and probably won't visit until after January 2021.